SHORT CIRCULAR

AROUN

BUXTON

by
JOHN N. MERRILL

Maps and photographs by John N. Merrill.

a J.N.M. PUBLICATION

1991

a J.N.M. PUBLICATION,

J.N.M. PUBLICATIONS,
WINSTER,
MATLOCK,
DERBYSHIRE.
DE4 2DQ
☎ *Winster (062988) 454*
FAX *Winster (062988) 416*

Conceived, edited, typeset, designed, paged, marketed and distributed by John N. Merrill.

© *Text and routes - John N. Merrill 1987 & 1991.*

© *Maps and photographs - John N. Merrill 1987 &1991.*

First Published - 1987

This edition - May 1991

ISBN 0 907496 57 1

Meticulous research has been undertaken to ensure that this publication is highly accurate at the time of going to press. The publishers, however, cannot be held responsible for alterations, errors or omissions, but they would welcome notification of such for future editions.

Typeset in - Plantin - bold, italic and plain 9pt and 18pt.

Printed by - Redwood Press Ltd., Melksham, Wilts.

Cover sketch - "Solomon's Temple, Grin Low, Buxton" by John Creber © J.N.M. PUBLICATIONS 1991.

An all British product.

Hi! - a few notes about Footslogger.

He was born in the flatlands around Luton in Bedfordshire, but his athletic capabilities soon showed themselves on Sports Day and in the football and cricket teams. Although expelled twice from different schools, he moved to Sheffield and was taken out into the Peak District at the age of 6 1/2. Here he ran up and down the rocks and the sense of enjoyment and freedom has never left him. He was hooked on the outdoors for life. By the age of 15 he had 350 books on the Himalayas and other mountain areas and although failed all eight O levels, he was writing a book on the history of mountaineering! At 16 he soloed the 90 foot high school building and the headmaster rushed him off to Outward Bound Mountain School to be properly trained - he thought it was a fantastic holiday!

At 17 he was chosen with eleven others to go on an expedition to Norway, for a month. Since then he has walked more than 100,000 miles in different parts of the world. He has walked The Cleveland Way 8 times; The Peakland Way 14 times; The Limey Way 14 times; The Pennine Way 4 times; Offa's Dyke 3 times; Pembrokeshire Coast Path 3 times; and all the other official paths at least twice.

He is an avid walker and never known to be really tired; likes to carry heavy loads at 18,000 feet and hates having his socks or shirts washed after a six month walk! His ideal day is a 25 mile walk with three bars of chocolate in his pocket. Having worn out nearly fifty pairs of boots he truly lives upto his nickname, Footslogger!

ERRWOOD RESERVOIR

CONTENTS —

THE CRESCENT

INTRODUCTION

With the Peak District National Park lying on its doorstep, Buxton makes an ideal base for exploring the western side of the area. My principal aim in this book is to illustrate the remarkably diverse walking to be found within seven miles of the town. Starting first with a town walk to explore its splendid architectural splendours and to see how the town has developed. The next walk, while skirting the town, ascends the hills above it providing views of Buxton's incomparable setting.

The subsequent walks take you into gritstone moorland country, with reservoirs, woodland and gritstone outcrops; especially the scenically attractive Goyt Valley. You explore the high tops as well as the valley floors. Another leads you from the second highest inn in the country to where three counties meets. Interlaced with them are many historical features and folklore.

To the south of Buxton are the limestone dales, a dramatic contrast to the rugged moors, being more gentle walking and softer landscape. Wild flowers abound and the villages have inns and numerous unspoilt cottages and field systems. From Earl Sterndale you explore the infant River Dove and walk beneath impressive limestone reef knolls.

Here are a few of my favourite walks in the Buxton area and I hope they give you as much as they have given me over the last few years.

Happy walking!

John N. Merrill

John N. Merrill (Footslogger)
Derbyshire. 1991

1

BUXTON FROM SOLOMON'S TEMPLE

ABOUT BUXTON......

Nestling in a bowl at 1,000 feet above sea level and surrounded by hills, Buxton is the highest borough and market town in England. The Romans named the town, Aquae Arnenetiae, and the healing properties of the local spa water were well known to them. Buxton is Derbyshire's major spa town and accounts for its early fame and many of its principal buildings. The spa water comes from seven springs and has a constant temperature of 82F and a daily flow rate of 200,000 gallons. The indoor swimming pool in the Pavilion Gardens uses the natural warm water.

Buxton's development can be seen clearly with the original area — Higher Buxton — complete with market place, stone cross and nearby St Anne's church, the oldest building in Buxton, dated late 16th century. The newer — Lower Buxton — is down the hill dominated by The Crescent, built by the fifth Duke of Devonshire in 1780-86 at a cost of £120,000 and designed by John Carr of York. The nearby Old Hall Hotel was rebuilt in 1670 and is renowned for the visits of Mary, Queen of Scots who stayed there in the 1570's to take Buxton Spa water. In the area are further very attractive buildings — the classical St John Church, the Devonshire Hospital built originally as the stables to The Crescent with one of the largest domes in the world, the Pavilion Gardens, the beautifully restored Opera House, and the impressive railway station window.

The unique Derbyshire custom of well dressing is carried out here in July together with a carnival. Today Buxton is a popular conference centre and base for exploring the surrounding Peak District National Park. The town hosts many fairs, conferences and artistic programmes in the Pavilion Gardens and Opera House. Many buildings have been renovated and, in keeping with the times, shopping malls are being constructed.

Early Closing Day — Wednesday.

Market Day — Tuesday, (Easter to December) Saturday.

BUXTON OPERA HOUSE

WHAT TO SEE/PLACES TO VISIT
—a random selection

Pavilion Gardens—covering 23 acres, with thermal spa fed swimming pool, conservatory and cafeteria. Tel. Buxton 23114.

Buxton Micrarium—opposite The Crescent; a unique museum revealing the natural world by microscope. Won a Special Judges Award in "Museum of the Year Awards" 1985. Tel. Buxton 78662.

Museum, on Terrace Road—important archaeological collection, many from the Derbyshire/Peak District area. Tel. Buxton 24658.

Buxton Railway Station—its window and Peak Rail Centre.

Pooles Cavern and adjoining Country Park—the cavern has daily tours into the passageways and was one of the 'seven wonders of the Peak; with stalactites and stalagmites and source of the Derbyshire River Wye. The park has 100 acres of woodland with paths leading to Solomon's Temple. Tel. Buxton 26978.

Corbar Cross—for extensive views over town.

High Edge Raceway—off A53 Buxton to Leek Road. Frequent race meets on one of Britain's largest raceways, including Hot Rods, Formula 1 Stockcars and Banger racing. Tel. Buxton 23674.

Buxton Opera House—extensive arts programme. Box Office Tel. Buxton 71010.

Tourist Information Centre, The Crescent. Tel. Buxton 71010.

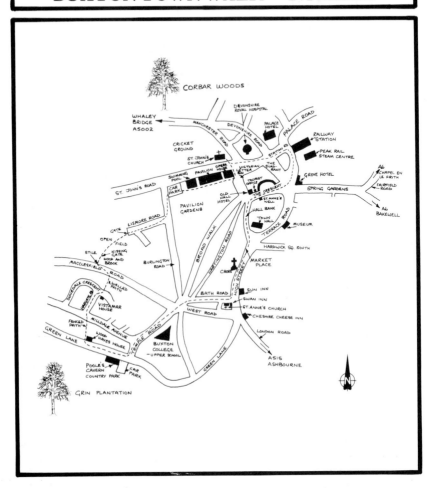

PAVILLION GARDENS

BUXTON — TOWN WALK — 2½ miles
— allow 2 hours

MAPS — O.S. 1:25,000 Outdoor Leisure series — The White Peak — West Sheet.
— O.S. 1:25,000 Pathfinder Series — Sheet No SK07/17 — Buxton.

CAR PARK: West side of Pavilion Gardens adjacent to St. John''s Road and Burlington Road.

ABOUT THE WALK — The original town is above The Crescent; known as Higher Buxton, where the Market and Cross still remain. Down the hill is the Georgian Buxton, with Crescent, Devonshire Hospital, unique spa swimming baths and Opera House. On this walk you'll explore the extensive Pavilion and Gardens and pass many of the Georgian buildings, before ascending to Higher Buxton and its remarkable St. Anne's Church. You cross to the southern fringe beneath Grin Plantation to see Poole's Cavern before weaving your way between houses and across fields to the car park.

WALKING INSTRUCTIONS — Walk to the end of the car park and join the tarmaced path through the Pavilion Gardens, passing the Swimming Pool and Pavilion on your left. Turn left at the end and pass the Opera House and cross St. John's Street to St. John's Church. Turn right and cross Manchester Road and pass the Devonshire Royal Hospital on your left before walking up Station Road to the Railway Station. Turn right and descend the No Through Road down to the Quadrant. Opposite the Grove Hotel, cross over and walk along The Crescent, passing the Crescent building on your right, before the Information Office and Old Hall Hotel. Bear left and ascend Hall Bank to the Market Place. Bear right and continue along into High Street. In front of the Swan Inn, turn right into Bath Road. On your left is St. Anne's Church.

Continue along Bath Road to Macclesfield Road. Cross over to your right and ascend Temple Road — footpath-signed for Poole's Cavern. Follow the road round to your right to Green Lane. Opposite is Poole's Cavern. Turn right and walk along Green Lane for 120 yards to Wood Hayes House on your right. Just past it on the right is the fenced path down to Milldale Avenue. Cross this to your right and descend Hargate Road. At the bottom, cross Dove Dale Crescent to your right and descend another fenced, then walled, path to the Macclesfield Road. Turn left then right almost immediately through the stone stile and follow the path through woodland to a kissing gate. Keep on the path across the open field to a gate at the end of Lismore Road. Walk along this road to Burlington Road, where turn left, and a short distance later on your right is the Pavilion Gardens and car park.

VICTORIAN POST BOX

5

HISTORICAL NOTES — IN WALKING ORDER

SWIMMING POOL — Opened in 1972, the main pool holds 140,000 gallons of Buxton Spa water. Buxton was a very fashionable Spa for many years, and the water is known for its therapeutic qualities. The spa water has never failed, and a constant 200,000 gallons a day issue forth at a constant temperature — summer and winter — of 82F.

PAVILION GARDENS — contain 23 acres of gardens and were opened in 1871. The buildings are good examples of Victorian design and workmanship. The Octagonal Hall was erected in 1875.

OPERA HOUSE — Built in 1903 at a cost of £25,000. Has recently been extensively restored, and contains several painted ceilings. Theatres and shows are held here all year round.

VICTORIAN LETTERBOX — Opposite the Opera House and made in 1867. The hexagonal box is known as the Penfield after the designer J.W. Penfield. There are only 101 left in the country, and this is the only one in Derbyshire.

ST. JOHN THE BAPTIST CHURCH — classical style, built in 1811 by Sir Jeffery Wyatville. Inside is an exceptional organ by William Hill in 1897, and the stained glass windows are of particular note.

DEVONSHIRE ROYAL HOSPITAL — Formerly the Great Stables for the Crescent, it was designed by John Carver. The dome, one of the largest in the world, covers a surface area of 50 yards in diameter.

PALACE HOTEL — Built in 1868 by the 7th Duke of Devonshire and designed by Henry Currey, it is believed to have cost £100,000.

ST. ANN'S WELL — Running spa water, which can be sampled and does not have the usual unsavoury spa water taste, and is one of the reasons why Buxton Spa water is so popular. The annual well-dressing ceremony takes place here in July.

OLD HALL HOTEL — One of the oldest buildings of Lower Buxton and was known as Buxton Hall, owned by the 6th Earl of Shrewsbury, George Talbot. He and his wife, Bess of Hardwick, were the "jailers" of Mary Queen of Scots. She came here several times to take the waters; the last time in 1584. The present building dates from 1670, and has a five-bay front with a Tuscan doorway.

MARKET CROSS — dates from the 15th Century; the stocks would have been close by.

ST. ANNE'S CHURCH — Oldest church in Buxton, being built in the 16th Century. The date 1625 on the porch refers to the porch only. The interior has a remarkable tiebeamed roof, with painted ceiling above the altar and a magnificent array of stained glass windows. To the rear of the churchyard is the tomb to John Kane. He died quite tragically in Buxton, and was a notable actor.

POOLE'S CAVERN — One of the Seven Wonders of the Peak (St. Anne's Well is another). Extensive show cave, floodlit throughout. Adjoining the site is 100 acres of woodland, now a country park. Footpaths lead to Solomon's Temple on Grin Low, half a mile away, providing extensive views over Buxton.

ST. JOHN THE BAPTIST CHURCH, BUXTON

THE DEVONSHIRE HOSPITAL

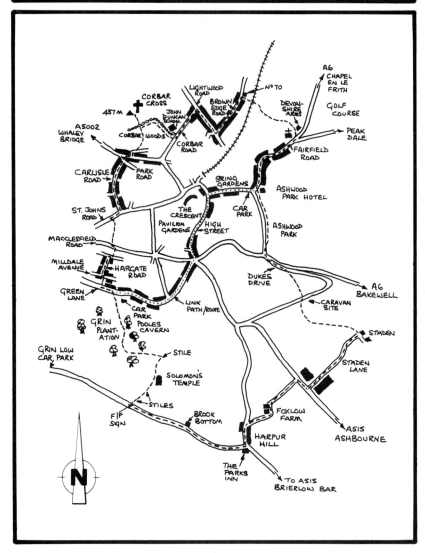

CORBAR CROSS

THE HILLS OF BUXTON

— complete walk — 8 miles; shorter walks 5 miles each. Allow 3½ or 2½ hours.

MAPS — O.S. 1:25,000 Outdoor Leisure Map — The White Peak (West Sheet) — O.S. 1:25,000 Pathfinder Series Sheet No. SK 07/17 — Buxton.

CAR PARK: 1. Beside the railway viaduct opposite the junction of Fairfield Road (A6) and Spring Gardens Road.
2. Pooles Cavern — Buxton Country Park.
3. Off route — Grin Low.

ABOUT THE WALK — Buxton, the highest market town in England at just over 1,000 feet above sea level, is surrounded by hills. From their summits you have exceptional views over the town and surrounding countryside. To the south is Solomon,s Temple standing in limestone country and in the north is Corbar Cross, in gritstone country. On the complete circuit you ascend both summits but can do half the circuit by ascending only one of them and using Green Lane, High Street and Spring Gardens roads as your link and return route — as detailed on the map. To reach the summits you ascend through woodland, traverse open fields, pass hamlets, places of historic interest, modern suburbia and industry.

WALKING INSTRUCTIONS — Starting the walk from the car park on Spring Gardens, cross the road into Fairfield Road and turn right past the Ashwood Park Hotel and into Ashwood Park. Keep the River Wye on your right as you walk through the park to the footbridge at the other end to the A6 road. Turn left to the traffic lights and bear right (not sharp right) onto Dukes Drive Road. Walk up here for about 100 yards to the second wooden gate on your right with a stile. Turn right and keep the wall on your left above a quarry to a gap in the next wall ahead. Bear right to a stile in the corner of the next field, close to the electricity pole. Descend with the wall on your right and caravan park opposite. Cross the road and walk up the drive, passing the gate pillars — Highlands. Continue bewteen the farm buildings and immediately turn left onto a walled track which you follow to the hamlet of Staden.

Turn right along the road and towards its junction with the A515 past the industrial estate. At the road turn right then left along the track to Foxlow Farm. Turn left through the buildings then right along the track and descend to the Harpur Hill Road. Turn left to the road junction in front of The Parks Inn and turn right along Grin Low Road. Follow it for the next½ mile first down to Brook Bottom then up the hill, ignoring the first path sign on your right and ¼ mile later at the next turn right and ascend to the prominent Solomon's Temple. Descend from the tower to a stile and continue descending a more prominent path. As you near the woodland turn left to a stile and follow the track beyond through the woodland. Ignore all side turnings and follow the track eventually round to your right. As you approach Poole's Cavern you can descend to your right down the steps to the car park and cavern entrance or keep left to the road — Green Lane. In both cases turn left along the road to House No 126 on your right. Here turn right along the fenced path.

At the end of the fenced path cross Milldale Avenue to your left and walk down Hargate Road. At the bottom turn right and left beside House No 26 along the fenced path to the B5059 Macclesfield Road. Turn left and just past House No 52 turn right onto the track and after a few yards keep ahead to the stile and path across the field to a minor road. Turn left to the A53 road — St. John's Road. Turn right and left and ascend Carlisle Road. At the top turn left along Park Road to the A5002 road. Turn right and almost immediately left onto the wooded path. You now continue ascending, heading from Corbar Cross. There are several paths here in Corbar Woods but remembering you have to ascend you should follow the correct one to the stile and open country beneath the cross. Ascend to the cross and return to the stile.

Back at the stile turn left along the path just inside the wall and woodland and follow it round and descend the steps to Corbar Road and John Duncan School on your left. Turn left along the road and follow it to its junction with Lightwood Road. Turn right and ¼ mile later turn left into Brown Edge Road. ¼ mile along here and where the road bends left, turn right onto the path in front of house No 70. The path soon descends and crosses the railway line via a bridge. Beyond bear right and follow the tarmaced path with the houses on your immediate right as you ascend towards Fairfield Church. Cross the churchyard to the Devonshire Arms. Turn right to the A6 — Fairfield Road. Descend this back to Ashwood Park and where you began.

SOLOMON'S TEMPLE — built by Solomon Mycock, who employed several local unemployed people in 1896.

CORBAR CROSS — Placed here in 1950 by the Roman Catholic church to commemorate Holy Year.

POOLE'S CAVERN — once one of the Seven Wonders of the Peak, and named after an outlaw called Poole who kept his spoils here. The cavern has an extensive cave system and guided parties leave throughout the day.

FAIRFIELD COTTAGES

ST. ANNE'S CHURCH

WILD MOOR

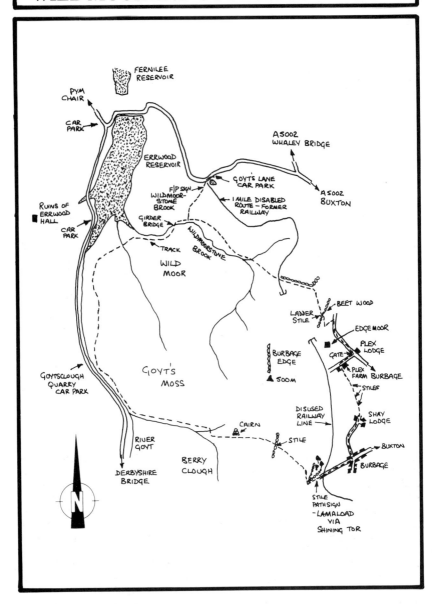

FERNILEE RESERVOIR

PYM CHAIR

CAR PARK

ERRWOOD RESERVOIR

A5002 WHALEY BRIDGE

GOYT'S LANE CAR PARK

F/P SIGN
WILDMOOR-STONE BROOK

1 MILE DISABLED ROUTE — FORMER RAILWAY

A5002 BUXTON

RUINS OF ERRWOOD HALL

CAR PARK

GIRDER BRIDGE

WILDMOORSTONE BROOK

TRACK

WILD MOOR

LADDER STILE

BEET WOOD

EDGE MOOR

BURBAGE EDGE

GATE

PLEX LODGE

500M

PLEX FARM BURBAGE

GOYTSCLOUGH QUARRY CAR PARK

GOYT'S MOSS

STILES

DISUSED RAILWAY LINE

SHAY LODGE

CAIRN

RIVER GOYT

BERRY CLOUGH

STILE

BUXTON

BURBAGE

DERBYSHIRE BRIDGE

STILE
PATH SIGN
– LAMALOAD
VIA
SHINING TOR

N

above the river and after ½ mile more gives views of Errwood Reservoir. You now keep a wall on your right as you begin curving round to your right and the path reaches a track. Follow this round into Wildmoorstone and descend to the brook crossed via a steel girder bridge. Turn right and in a few yards regain your starting out path on your left. Turn left and ascend back to the disused railway line and car park just beyond.

WILD MOOR AND GOYT MOSS — 7 miles — allow 3 hours

ROUTE — Goyt Lane Car Park — Wildmoorstone Brook — Beet Wood — Plex Farm — Shay Lodge — Burbage — Goyt's Moss — Wild Moor — Goyt Lane Car Park.

MAPS — O.S. 1:25,000 Outdoor Leisure Map — The White Peak (West Sheet). — O.S. 1:25,000 Pathfinder Series Sheet No. SK 07/17 — Buxton.

CAR PARK — Goyt Lane Car Park. — Goytsclough Quarry.

ABOUT THE WALK — The toughest walk in the book, being remote with several ascents, but one of the most enjoyable! The walk encircles the moorland around Burbage Edge providing stunning views over moorland and Errwood Reservoir in the west and eastwards over Buxton and its hills. Whilst the walk starts from Goyts Lane car park, it is possible to start from Goytsclough Quarry car park.

WALKING INSTRUCTIONS — Turn left out of the car park onto the road and walk past the old railway line on your left; now a one mile route for the disabled. Just ahead leave the road at the path sign — Wildstonemoor Brook — and descend the narrow path to the path junction above the brook. Turn left along the defined path and begin ascending gently up the wide valley, passing a path sign — Burbage — after a few yards. The path is defined and regularly marked with wooden posts. A little over ½ mile you reach the disused railway line, close to the sealed tunnel on your right. Continue ahead with a wall on your left onto the summit of the moorland. Where the wall turns left you bear right and descend to a ladder stile beside Beet Wood. Descend to your right then left to gain the walled track reached by a stile beside a path sign.

Turn right along the track past the lodge and along the drive of Edgemoor to the white gates and Plex Lodge on your left. Turn right up the walled track to Plex Farm and take the second gate on your left and walk through the farmyard on a track and across the subsequent field to a stone stile. Continue ahead to another stile and descend on the path through the trees to the next stile. Keep the wall on your left as you head for Shay Lodge. Here you gain a walled track which you follow straight ahead to the road on the western edge of Burbage. Turn right up the road which soon becomes a track. Shortly after passing the disused railway line, turn right at the stile and footpath sign on your right — "Lamaload via Shining Tor" with plaque in memory of Jack and Mary Gyte. The path at first keeps close to the wall and woodland on your right before swinging right and leaving the woodland as you ascend to the top righthand corner of the field to a stile. Over this and you return to moorland again as you at first keep level for a little over ¼ mile to a cairn. After this the path descends, crossing a side stream before walking down Berry Clough.

At the bottom, instead of crossing the bridge over the Goyt River, turn right along the defined path above it. In a little over ½ mile pass the footbridge on your left which gives access to Goytsclough Quarry. Keep on the path as it winds its way high

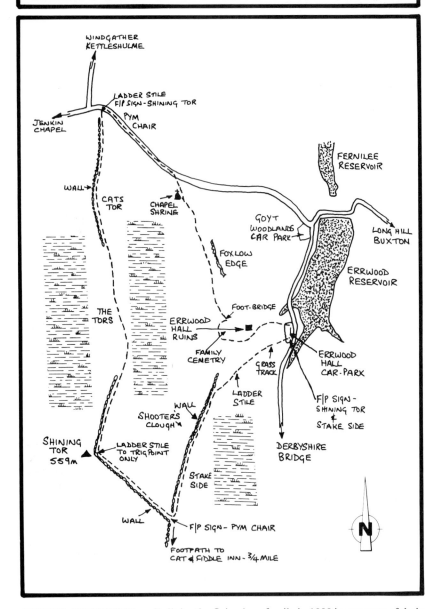

CIRCULAR SHRINE — Built by the Grimshaw family in 1889 in memory of their Spanish governess. The shrine is dedicated to St. Joseph.

ERRWOOD RESERVOIR — Completed in 1967 for the Stockport and District Water Board, and has a holding capacity of 927 million gallons. The neighbouring Fernilee Reservoir was completed in 1938 and has a capacity of 1,087 million gallons.

ERRWOOD AND SHINING TOR — 6 MILES
— allow 2½ hours

ROUTE — Errwood Hall car park — Stake Side — Shining Tor — The Tors —
Cats Tor — Pym Chair — Errwood Shrine — Errwood Hall (ruins) — car park.

MAPS — O.S. 1:25,000 Outdoor Leisure Map — The White Peak — west sheet.
— O.S. 1:25,000 Pathfinder Series — Sheet No SK07/17 — Buxton.

CAR PARK — Errwood Hall

ABOUT THE WALK — a high moorland walk which is best appreciated in good
weather to visibly see the route and enjoy the extensive views. A very short walk can
be made to explore the grounds and ruins of Errwood Hall. The walk can be
extended from the path junction near Shining Tor to visit the Cat and Fiddle Inn —
one of the highest in the country — 3/4 mile away. The walk from Shining Tor is
down a broad ridge with impressive views and is basically downhill all the way back
to Errwood Hall car park. The hardest part is the initial ascent to Shining Tor.

WALKING INSTRUCTIONS — From the lefthand side (southern end) of the car
park pick up the signed path — Shining Tor and Stake Side. The path is well defined
and soon becomes a grass track as you ascend gradually, with woodland on your left.
After almost ½ mile ascend a ladder stile and soon gain a wall on your right. Keep
close to this as you bear left continuing your ascent up the shoulder of Stake Side.
Over the wall and below is Shooter's Clough. After nearly a mile beside the wall
reach a footpath junction. The path ahead is to the Cat and Fiddle Inn and the path
on your right, as signed — Pym Chair — leads you towards the summit of Shining
Tor. Keep the wall on your left to the summit. Access to the triangulation pillar is via
the stile.

Continue along the path with the wall on your left as you now gently descend along
the ridge over The Tors and Cats Tor to the road at Pym Chair, 1½ miles away. Turn
right along the road for ½ mile before turning right onto the path and continue
descending beneath Foxlow Edge, passing the small circular shrine on your right.
The path is well defined for the next ¾ mile with the stream on your right. After ¾
mile turn right over the footbridge and ascend the path, which soon joins a track
where you turn left down it. Just off to your left is the Grimshawe cemetery. After
200 yards the track divides; to your left round the corner are the ruins of Errwood
Hall. The one ahead continues through the rhododendrons, which are particularly
attractive in June when in full bloom. After a few yards bear right at the next
junction and you soon emerge into the field above the car park. Descend back to
your starting point.

ERRWOOD HALL — built by Samuel Grimshaw in 1830, whose estate covered
496 acres. The Grimshaws planted over 40,000 azaleas and rhododendrons in the
area and accounts for the extensive foliage today. The building was Italian style with
a large central tower. In 1930 the building was purchased by Stockport Corporation
and for a short while served as a Youth Hostel before being pulled down in 1934 with
the building of Fernilee Reservoir.

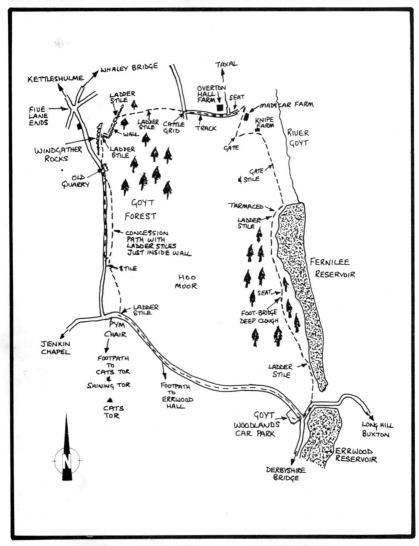

RUINS OF ERRWOOD HALL

FERNILEE AND WINDGATHER — 6 MILES
— allow 2½ hours.

ROUTE — Goyt Woodlands car park — Fernilee Reservoir — Knipe Farm — Madscar Farm — Overton Hall Farm — Windgather Rocks — Pym Chair — car park.

MAPS — O.S. 1:25,000 Outdoor Leisure Map — The White Peak — west sheet. — O.S. 1:25,000 Pathfinder Series — Sheet No SK07/17 — Buxton.

CAR PARK — Goyt Woodlands

ABOUT THE WALK — A delightful walk, first through the forest above Fernilee Reservoir before ascending past farms and through more woodland to the impressive gritstone outcrop — Windgather Rocks. You return down the road from Pym Chair back to the car park. The walk can be extended from this road by 1½ miles to include a visit to the ruins of Errwood Hall surrounded by rhododendrons. This diversion is detailed in the Errwood & Shining Tor walk. A short road walk (northwards) will return you to the Goyt Woodlands car park.

WALKING INSTRUCTIONS — From the car park return to the road and turn left to the start of the dam wall of Errwood Reservoir. Here leave the road and descend on a faint path to the one close to the shores of Fernilee Reservoir. You soon enter woodland, and after ¼ mile at Jep Clough ascend a ladder stile and ascend away from the reservoir on a well defined path. Little over ¼ mile later cross a footbridge over Deep Clough. ½ mile later ascend a ladder stile, and at the end of the trees bear right on a tarmaced road to the start of the dam wall of Fernilee Reservoir. Here turn left on the track and after ¼ mile pass through a stile and ¼ mile later ignore the track to Normanwood on your left. Ascend gently to Knipe Farm and ignore two rights of way to your left and keep on the track that ascends above Mill Clough, where it turns sharp right and continues ascending above Madscar Farm. Just after is another sharp bend, and here follow it round to your left to pass a seat on your right and just after Overton Hall Farm. Continue up the farm road to the road.

Cross over and follow a faint path at first as you ascend directly up moorland with Goyt Forest on your left. Just over the top of the rise gain the forest edge and ladder stile. Ascend into the trees following the path through them to another ladder stile, ¼ mile away. Over this turn left beside the wall and follow the path to another ladder stile. Over this you are close to the top of Windgather Rocks. Turn left along the top to gain the minor road. Continue along the road (due south) for ½ mile. There is a concessionary path just over the wall on your left with ladder stiles. After ½ mile gain a stile and bear left diagonally across the moorland on a path to the road near Pym Chair. Opposite to your right is the path to Shining Tor. Turn left down the road and 1¼ miles later gain Goyt Woodlands car park. After ½ mile you can leave the road and follow the path to Errwood Hall as an extension.

COMBS RESERVOIR — 3 MILES

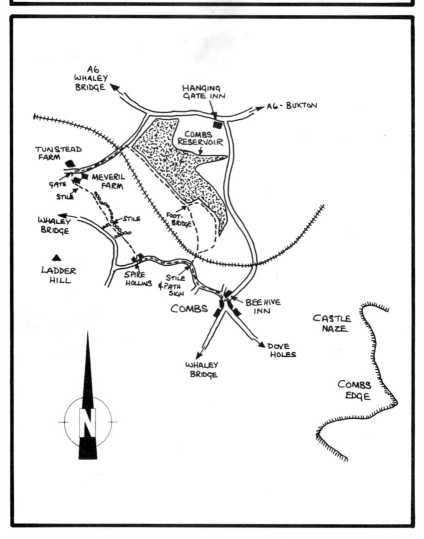

FOOTBRIDGE, NR. COMBS RESERVOIR

COMBS RESERVOIR — 3 MILES
— 1½ hours

ROUTE — Combs — Combs Reservoir — Meveril Farm — Spire Hollins Farm — Combs.

MAPS — O.S. 1:25,000 Outdoor Leisure Map — The White Peak (West Sheet). — O.S. 1:25,000 Pathfinder Series Sheet No. SK 07/17 — Buxton.

CAR PARK — no official one

ABOUT THE WALK — Starting from an attractive village dominated by the edge of Combs Moss, this short walk takes you along the shore of Combs Reservoir before ascending above it providing distant views over the area. The reservoir is used to feed the nearby Peak Forest Canal that starts at Whaley Bridge. Near Meveril Farm, Tunstead Farm is associated with one of the most intriguing Peak District legends — the skull, Dickey o' Tunstead.

WALKING INSTRUCTIONS — The walk begins in the centre of Combs, facing the Beehive Inn. Walk along the road to the left of the inn following it round to your right for ¼ mile. Where it turns sharp left, is a stile and path sign on your right. Turn right here and pass through the railway tunnel. There is a path to your right which leads to the shores of the reservoir, where you turn left along it. Another path is to your left across the field with holly hedge on your right to a stile. Through this continue across the next field and through the sparse hedge to a wooden footbridge. Turn left along the path beside the reservoir. The other path leads you into this. Walk beside the reservoir for a little over ½ mile to the dam wall and minor road. Turn left and ascend the road to Meveril Farm. Take the second gate on your left to walk above the top farm to a stile. Continue on a grass track, and where it ascends the hillside bear left close to the wall on your left, now on a faint path. Gain another stile and at the end of the next field a gap in the wall, before descending towards Spire Hollins Farm. Gain the track and follow it round to a high stone stile, signposted — footpath —, on your right. Ascend this and walk between the house and garage to a wrought iron gate. Continue past the house — Spire Hollins, to the road. Turn left and follow the road back past your earlier path back into central Combs, ½ mile away.

BEE HIVE INN — The present inn was built in 1863. The original inn of the same name was at right angles to the present one.

DICKEY O'TUNSTEAD — Known as the restless skull, for on many occasions the 350 year old skull has been moved; even buried in the churchyard of Chapel-en-le-Frith's church. On each occasion many unexplained things of happened until it was brought back to Tunstead Farm.

DANEBOWER AND THREE SHIRE HEADS – 7 MILES

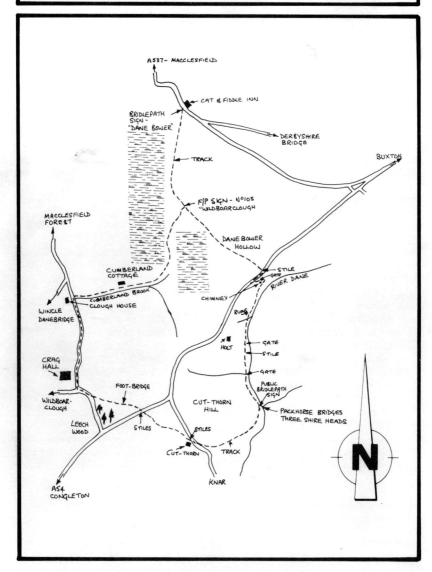

CAT & FIDDLE INN — At 1,690 feet a.s.l. the inn is the second highest in the country. In 1831 the inn was a newly erected and well accustomed inn or public house. Mystery still prevails as to how it was so named, although the Sixth Duke of Devonshire, in 1857, gave the landlord a photograph of a cat and fiddle.

THREE SHIRE HEADS — Where the counties of Staffordshire, Cheshire and Derbyshire meet. The bridges are the remains of the important packhorse routes that once crossed the area. One of the pools here is aptly named — "Panniers Pool."

DANEBOWER AND THREE SHIRE HEADS
— 7 MILES
— allow 3 hours

ROUTE — Cat & Fiddle — Dane Bower — A54 — River Dane — Three Shire Heads — Cut-Thorn — Leech Wood — Crag Hall — Cumberland Brook — Cat & Fiddle.

MAPS — O.S. 1;25,000 Outdoor Leisure Map — The White Peak — west sheet. — O.S. 1:25,000 Pathfinder Series — Sheet No SK07/17 — Buxton.

CAR PARK — opposite Cat & Fiddle Inn.

ABOUT THE WALK — Starting from one of the highest inns in the country, you cross extensive moorland before descending to the infant River Dane and the packhorse bridges at Three Shire Heads. Here you ascend and cross fields to reach the edge of Wildboarclough and Crag Hall. A short road walk brings you to Cumberland Brook, where you ascend back onto the moorland and retrace your starting out path. A very attractive and remote walk in stunning scenery.

WALKING INSTRUCTIONS — Opposite the Cat & Fiddle Inn join the well defined track at the bridlepath sign — "Dane Bower". Follow this over the moorland for ¾ mile to path sign — No 105 — Wildboarclough via Cumberland Brook. This is your return path. Continue on the track and soon begin descending Dane Bower Hollow to the A54 road. Turn right, and after 75 yards, left on the track. After a few yards pass through a gate and shortly afterwards a chimney on your right. Just past this descend to your right diagonally down to the infant River Dane. You now keep the river on your left for the next mile to the packhorse bridges at Three Shire Heads. The path is sometimes faint but all the stiles and gates are there as you head almost due south.

At the bridges don't cross over but follow the track which gradually ascends and curves round Cut-thorn Hill. Little over ½ mile you gain the tarmaced road beside Cut-thorn House. On the right of it is the stile and your next path. The path is defined as you cross two fields to reach the A54 road again after ½ mile. Cross over and follow the path, first to a footbridge and then down the field to its far righthand corner with Leech Wood on your left. A few more yards and you reach the Wildboarclough road. Turn right along it to the road junction a few yards later. Turn right passing Crag Hall on your left and keep on the road for the next ¾ mile until almost opposite Clough House on your left. Turn right just before it at Footpath sign No. 104 — Cat & Fiddle. Follow the track and after 150 yards cross the Cumberland Brook and continue on the track with the brook and trees on your right. ½ mile from the bridge, pass through a gate and continue ahead on a track and begin to ascend up Danethorn Hollow as you bear left. The ascent is steep and after ¼ mile gain a wall on your left. Continue on the path on the right of it as you ascend more gently in moorland back to footpath No 105. Turn left and retrace your steps back to the Cat & Fiddle.

KING STERNDALE AND WOOD DALE — 4½ MILES

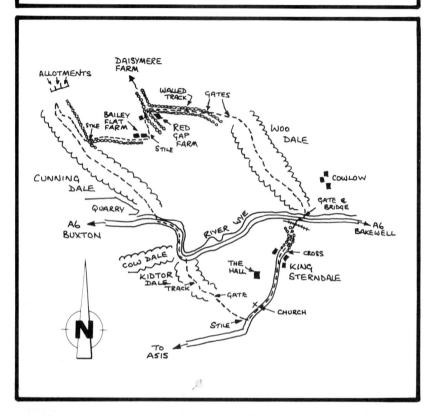

KING STERNDALE CROSS

KING STERNDALE AND WOO DALE

— 4½ miles — allow 2 hours

ROUTE — King Sterndale — Church — Kidtor Dale — A6 — Cunning Dale — Bailey Flat Farm — Red Gap Farm — Woo Dale — A6 — King Sterndale.

MAPS — 1;25,000 O.S. Outdoor Leisure Map — The White Peak — west sheet. — O.S. 1:S5,000 Pathfinder Series Sheet No. SK 07/17 — Buxton.

CAR PARK: no official one

ABOUT THE WALK — King Sterndale at the end of a No Through Road is an exceptionally secluded hamlet with a common and remains of a cross. This hilly walk is full of surprises with the unspoilt Kidtor Dale, the long shallow Cunning Dale and the deeper and broader Woo Dale. It is a delightful walk in quiet limestone dales, away from the more popular haunts.

WALKING INSTRUCTIONS —Starting from the centre of King Sterndale, walk southwards along the road for ¼ mile passing the church on your right. A few yards later turn right at the gate and ascend the stile just ahead. Walk across the field passing the walled tree enclosures on your right. Approaching the end of the field bear right to a gate and gain a track in woodland. Follow this well-cut track as you descend past limestone buttresses to the A6 road. Turn left along it and pass under the railway bridge, and a little further leave it and cross the River Wye, at the entrance to Tarmac's Quarry. Ascend the track, and where it turns sharp left continue ahead on a footpath along the floor of Cunning Dale. Ascend gradually for ¾ mile to the top of the dale. Here turn sharp right onto the path, almost doubling back on yourself, that ascends the dale side. Keep on the path beneath the top of the dale side to a stile and 150 yards later a stile in the wall on your left. Ascend this leaving the dale and keep the wall on your right to reach the stiles and Bailey Flat Farm.

Walk partly through the farm to the cow shed on your left. Here turn left to the stile and continue ascending close to the wall on your right to the crest of the field before descending to a barn opposite Red Gap Farm. Turn left along the track then right almost immediately as path signed and walk along the track for ¼ mile to a gate and where the track turns right. Here leave the track to your left and follow a grass track to a gate. Here turn right into Woo Dale and descend this for ¾ mile to the A6 road. Turn right, and 30 yards later left, and ascend the defined path to the ladder stile and railway line. Cross this and continue ascending steeply to a gate and track. Turn left along it back into King Sterndale.

CHELMORTON AND DEEP DALE — 4½ MILES

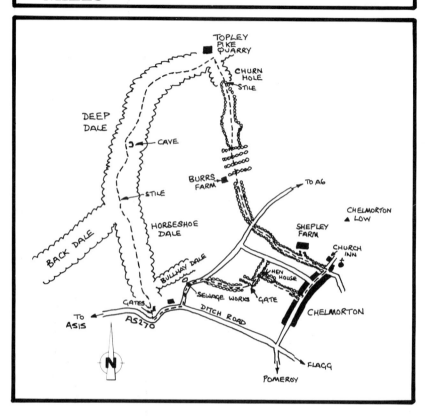

DEEP DALE

CHELMORTON AND DEEP DALE — 4½ miles — allow 2 hours

ROUTE — Chelmorton — Old Coalpit Lane — Churn Hole — Deep Dale — Horseshoe Dale — Chelmorton.

MAPS — O.S. 1:25,000 Outdoor Leisure Map — The White Peak — west sheet. — O.S. 1:25,000 Pathfinder Series Sheet No. SK 07/17 — Buxton.

CAR PARK: no official one

ABOUT THE WALK — Chelmorton is one of the highest villages in England — 1,200 feet a.s.l. — and often cut off in wintertime. This walk takes you from the village to one of the finest and dramatic limesone dales in the Peak District — Deep Dale. It is rugged in places but the scenery makes the effort well worthwhile. You ascend to the limestone plateau via the shallow Horseshoe Dale and cross the fields back to Chelmorton.

WALKING INSTRUCTIONS — Starting just down from the church and Church Inn in Chelmorton, turn right (if looking down the village) at the footpath sign — Old Coalpit Lane ½ mile. Keep on this track for ½ mile to the road. Cross over to your right (not left) onto a walled grass track — heading almost due north. After ¼ mile you leave the walled track behind as you near Burrs Farm. Keep to your right as guided by the stiles and continue to head to more stiles and into a large field. Keep to the base of it to the far righthand corner and stile. Keep the wall on your right all the way to the next stile and the steep short descent to Churn Hole. Descend the dale to near the quarry workings and turn left onto the defined path which ascends at first but soon levels out as you leave the quarry spoils and enter the rugged dale. The path is well defined as you keep to the lefthand side of Deep Dale, reaching its deep cave in ¾ mile.

Continue along the dale floor for almost ½ mile to a stile. Shortly afterwards bear left into Horseshoe Dale and ascend this for ¾ mile to the A5270 road, reached through a small farmyard. Turn left along the road and at the first road junction left along the road — still the A5270 road. Pass a small sewage works on your left as you round a righthand bend. Just afterwards turn right into a walled track and follow this to its end beside ruins on your right. Cross the next field to your left to a gate and gain another walled track. Keep ahead for a few yards to a hen house on your right. Just before it turn right through the gate and keep the wall on your right to the next stile. Continue ahead to the stiles and gain the main street in Chelmorton. Turn left to reach the church and inn.

CHELMORTON — The highest village in Derbyshire. The field enclosures are a classic example of late 18th century layout. The church dedicated to St. John the Baptist is mostly 15th century with a rare stone chancel screen. The wind vane on the spire is a grasshopper.

DEEP DALE CAVE — 70 feet long and said to the home of Hob Hirst.

EARL STERNDALE AND HOLLINSCLOUGH —6 MILES

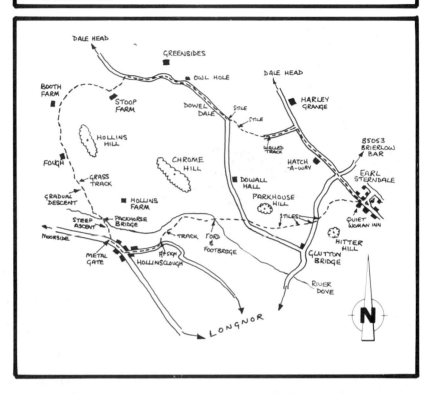

THE QUIET WOMAN, EARL STERNDALE

EARL STERNDALE AND HOLLINSCLOUGH
— 6 miles
— allow 2½ hours

ROUTE — Earl Sterndale — Hatch-a-way — Dowel Dale — Owl Hole — Stoop Farm — Booth Farm — Fough — Hollinsclough — River Dove — Hitter Hill — Earl Sterndale.

MAPS — O.S. 1:25,000 Outdoor Leisure Map — The White Peak (West Sheet). — O.S. 1:25,000 Pathfinder Series Sheet No. SK 07/17 — Buxton.

CAR PARK — no official one.

ABOUT THE WALK — Starting from the Quiet Woman Inn in Earl Sterndale, the walk takes you through some of the most dramatic limestone scenery in the Peak District. First you keep high up before descending to Hollinsclough and its views of the limestone reef knolls of Chrome Hill, Parkhouse Hill and Hitter Hill. You walk near the infant River Dove before the final ascent back to Earl Sterndale. A hilly but remarkably attractive walk along some of the lesser known paths in the area.

WALKING INSTRUCTIONS — Starting from the Quiet Woman Inn in Earl Sterndale, descend the road to the crossroads. Continue ahead on the road signposted — Dale Head, and ascend at first before levelling off as you pass the attractive Hatch-a-way Cottage on your left. Just over ¼ mile turn left onto the first track on your left. Keep on this for ¼ mile to a gate where the track turns left. Keep ahead over the stile and cross the large field, keeping the wall well to your right. After ¼ mile ascend a stone stile, near the righthand corner of the field, and descend abruptly to the minor road through Dowel Dale.

Turn right and ascend the road for ½ mile to the limestone — Owl Hole on your right. Continue on the road to a gate and bear left at the entrance to Greensides Farm. Go through another gate, and 150 yards later, where the track bears right at a yellow gritting box, turn left on the track to Stoop Farm. Where it descends to your left, leave the track and bear towards the righthand side of the trees and walk between the widely-spaced walls above the farm. After 150 yards you reach another track, which you follow to the entrance of Booth Farm ¼ mile away. Continue on the track — not to the farm — and in ¼ mile reach the house, Fough. Continue ahead on a grass track as you gently descend for ½ mile. Near the bottom bear right keeping a wall on your left to gain a small packhorse bridge over the infant River Dove. Ascend the defined path to the minor road, ¼ mile away, gained via a small metal gate. Turn left and descend into Hollinsclough.

In the centre of the village turn left passing the school on your left. ¼ mile later take the first track on your left, with upright footpath sign and barn. Follow the track for ¾ mile keeping near the River Dove on your left for half the time. After crossing a ford/footbridge gain the tarmaced road near Stannery on your right. Keep ahead on the road and, when opposite a stile on your right painted yellow, leave the road and although pathless begin crossing the large field bearing slightly left to reach a stile, with the slopes of Parkhouse Hill on your left. Continue ahead a little further before bearing right and descending to a stile and another just beyond to reach the road near Glutton Bridge. Cross to the next stile and begin the final and steep but short ascent angling to your left to the yellow-painted stile. Continue ascending the slopes of Hitter Hill to the next stile where the ascending ends. The path, which is well stiled, bears to your right across the fields to enter Earl Sterndale at the Quiet Woman Inn.

QUIET WOMAN INN — The inn sign depicts a headless woman about whom several legends are told. The most popular says the landlady was a chatterbox and in the end the villagers could stand it no longer and told the landlord to cut her head off. He did, and her gravestone warns others of a similar fate!

CHROME HILL

WOO DALE

28

CAT & FIDDLE INN

ERRWOOD SHRINE

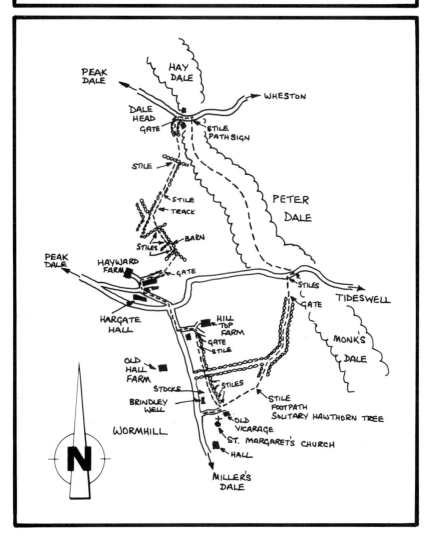

WORMHILL — The hall dates from 1697 and was the former home of the Bagshawe family, a prominent Derbyshire family. The church was built in 1864 and William Bagshawe, "The Apostle of the Peak", gave his first sermon here. The well is in memory of James Brindley, the canal engineer, who was born in the parish at Tunstead in 1716.

WORMHILL & PETER DALE — 4½ miles
— allow 2 hours

ROUTE — Wormhill — Wormhill Hill — Hargatewall — Dale Head — Peter Dale — Wormhill.

MAPS — O.S. 1:25,000 Outdoor Leisure Map — The White Peak (West Sheet) — O.S. 1:25,000 Pathfinder Series Sheet No. SK 07/17 — Buxton.

CAR PARK — No official one in Wormhill.

ABOUT THE WALK — Wormhill is a secluded but fascinating limestone village, with impressive church, magnificent hall, old stocks and a well in memory of James Brindley, the canal engineer born nearby. The walk takes you across the limestone plateau to Hargatewall where you descend to the head of Peter Dale. You walk through the delightful limestone dale before ascending back to Wormhill. The walk starts and ends at Wormhill church.

WALKING INSTRUCTIONS — Continue past the church gate and Old Vicarage on your right, to the path sign on your left. Turn left onto the fenced path to the next sign a few yards later. The path to your right to the solitary tree at the top of the field is the route you will be returning on. Keep ahead, as path signed, to the stone stile. For the next few fields to Hill Top Farm, you basically keep straight ahead and you will gain all the stiles. Cross a grass walled track and continue ahead with the wall on your immediate right. Gain the drive/track of Hill Top Farm via a small gate and turn left along the drive to the minor road. Turn right and at the cross roads keep straight ahead along the minor road which bears left, passing the northern end of Hargate Hall as you descend to Hargatewall. In the bottom turn right and take the second track on your right, passing the houses on your right and a water reservoir on your left. Keep on the walled track to a gate and onto another where you enter a large field. Keep ahead to the far end to a stile beside a gate. Don't cross this, but turn left to a stile on your left. The next few stiles are where the walls join. Pass a ruined barn on your right and two stiles to gain a large field. Keep ahead to a track and walled track on your left. Turn right on the track with wall on your left as you descend towards Peter Dale. After the next stile the wall is on your right. At the next stile you are above the dale and turn left to keep above it and reach a walled track which you descend to a gate and minor road at Dale Head Farm.

Turn right, and after a few yards right again, at the stile and path sign — Millers Dale. You now walk along the floor of Peter Dale for the next mile to the minor road between Hargatewall and Tideswell. At the road turn right, and left a few yards later, and ascend steeply the well defined path to a gate and walled track. Keep on this, ascending, for the next ½ mile to a stile and gate where the walled track divides. Take the left one, and where it ends keep ahead to the solitary hawthorn tree, which you saw at the beginning. Here is the stile. Turn right and continue along the field to the path sign you were at at the beginning. Turn left and retrace your steps back to the road beside Wormhill Church.

PETER DALE

EQUIPMENT NOTES — some personsal thoughts

BOOTS — preferably with a full leather upper, of medium weight, with a vibram sole. I always add a foam cushioned insole to help cushion the base of my feet.

SOCKS — I generally wear two thick pairs as this helps minimise blisters. The inner pair are of loop stitch variety and approximately 80% wool. The outer are a thick rib pair of approximately 80% wool.

WATERPROOFS — for general walking I wear a T shirt or shirt with a cotton wind jacket on top. You generate heat as you walk and I prefer to layer my clothes to avoid getting too hot. Depending on the season will dictate how many layers you wear. In soft rain I just use my wind jacket for I know it quickly dries out. In heavy downpours I slip on a neoprene lined cagoule, and although hot and clammy it does keep me reasonably dry. Only in extreme conditions will I don overtrousers, much preferring to get wet and feel comfortable.

FOOD — as I walk I carry bars of chocolate, for they provide instant energy and are light to carry. In winter a flask of hot coffee is welcome. I never carry water and find no hardship from doing so, but this is a personal matter! From experience I find the more I drink the more I want and sweat. You should always carry some extra food such as Kendal mint cake, for emergencies.

RUCKSACKS — for day walking I use a climbing rucksac of about 40 litre capacity and although excess space it does mean that the sac is well padded, an internal frame and padded shoulder straps. Inside apart from the basics for the day I carry gloves, balaclava, spare pullover and a pair of socks.

MAP & COMPASS — when I am walking I always have the relevant map — preferably the 1:25,000 scale — open in my hand. This enables me to constantly check that I am walking the right way. In case of bad weather I carry a compass, which once mastered gives you complete confidence in thick cloud or mist.

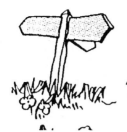

REMEMBER AND OBSERVE THE COUNTRY CODE

 Enjoy the countryside and respect its life and work.

 Guard against all risk of fire.

 Fasten all gates.

 Keep your dogs under close control.

 Keep to public paths across farmland.

 Use gates and stiles to cross fences, hedges and walls.

  Leave livestock, crops and machinery alone.

 Take your litter home - pack it in; pack it out.

 Help to keep all water clean.

Protect wildlife, plants and trees.

Take special care on country roads.

JAMES BRINDLEY WELL, WORMHILL

WALK RECORD CHART

Date Walked

BUXTON TOWN WALK — 2½ MILES..

THE HILLS OF BUXTON — 5 AND 8 MILES ....

WILD MOOR AND GOYT MOSS — 7 MILES ....

ERRWOOD AND SHINING TOR — 6 MILES ....

FERNILEE AND WINDGATHER — 6 MILES ....

COMBS RESERVOIR — 3 MILES ....

DANEBOWER AND THREE SHIRE HEADS — 7 MILES.........................

KING STERNDALE AND WOOD DALE — 4½ MILES............................

CHELMORTON AND DEEP DALE — 4½ MILES ....

EARL STERNDALE AND HOLLINSCLOUGH — 6 MILES ....

WORMHILL AND PETER DALE — 4½ MILES ....

GET A JOHN MERRILL SHORT WALK BADGE - Complete six of these walks and send a copy of the Walk Record Chart and £2.25 payable to JNM PUBLICATIONS for a signed certificate and badge - 3 1/2" diameter and four colour embroidered on a blue cloth.

"I'VE DONE A JOHN WALK" - T SHIRT - £5.75. all sizes - emerald green with white lettering.

OTHER BOOKS by
JOHN N. MERRILL
PUBLISHED by
JNM PUBLICATIONS

CIRCULAR WALK GUIDES -
SHORT CIRCULAR WALKS IN THE PEAK DISTRICT
LONG CIRCULAR WALKS IN THE PEAK DISTRICT
CIRCULAR WALKS IN WESTERN PEAKLAND
SHORT CIRCULAR WALKS IN THE STAFFORDSHIRE MOORLANDS
SHORT CIRCULAR WALKS AROUND THE TOWNS & VILLAGES OF
THE PEAK DISTRICT
SHORT CIRCULAR WALKS AROUND MATLOCK
SHORT CIRCULAR WALKS IN THE DUKERIES
SHORT CIRCULAR WALKS IN SOUTH YORKSHIRE
SHORT CIRCULAR WALKS IN SOUTH DERBYSHIRE
SHORT CIRCULAR WALKS AROUND BUXTON
SHORT CIRCULAR WALKS IN THE HOPE VALLEY
40 SHORT CIRCULAR WALKS IN THE PEAK DISTRICT
CIRCULAR WALKS ON KINDER & BLEAKLOW
SHORT CIRCULAR WALKS IN SOUTH NOTTINGHAMSHIRE
SHIRT CIRCULAR WALKS IN CHESHIRE
SHORT CIRCULAR WALKS IN WEST YORKSHIRE

CANAL WALKS -
VOL 1 - DERBYSHIRE & NOTTINGHAMSHIRE
VOL 2 - CHESHIRE & STAFFORDSHIRE
VOL 3 - STAFFORDSHIRE
VOL 4 - THE CHESHIRE RING
VOL 5 - LINCOLNSHIRE & NOTTINGHAMSHIRE
VOL 6 - SOUTH YORKSHIRE
VOL 7 - THE TRENT & MERSEY CANAL

JOHN MERRILL DAY CHALLENGE WALKS -
WHITE PEAK CHALLENGE WALK
DARK PEAK CHALLENGE WALK
PEAK DISTRICT END TO END WALKS
STAFFORDSHIRE MOORLANDS CHALLENGE WALK
THE LITTLE JOHN CHALLENGE WALK
YORKSHIRE DALES CHALLENGE WALK
NORTH YORKSHIRE MOORS CHALLENGE WALK
LAKELAND CHALLENGE WALK
THE RUTLAND WATER CHALLENGE WALK
MALVERN HILLS CHALLENGE WALK
INSTRUCTION & RECORD -
HIKE TO BE FIT.....STROLLING WITH JOHN
THE JOHN MERRILL WALK RECORD BOOK

MULTIPLE DAY WALKS -
THE RIVERS'S WAY
PEAK DISTRICT: HIGH LEVEL ROUTE
PEAK DISTRICT MARATHONS
THE LIMEY WAY
THE PEAKLAND WAY

COAST WALKS & NATIONAL TRAILS -
ISLE OF WIGHT COAST PATH
PEMBROKESHIRE COAST PATH
THE CLEVELAND WAY

PEAK DISTRICT HISTORICAL GUIDES -
A to Z GUIDE OF THE PEAK DISTRICT
DERBYSHIRE INNS - an A to Z guide
HALLS AND CASTLES OF THE PEAK DISTRICT & DERBYSHIRE
TOURING THE PEAK DISTRICT & DERBYSHIRE BY CAR
DERBYSHIRE FOLKLORE
PUNISHMENT IN DERBYSHIRE
CUSTOMS OF THE PEAK DISTRICT & DERBYSHIRE
WINSTER - a souvenir guide
ARKWRIGHT OF CROMFORD
TALES FROM THE MINES by Geoffrey Carr
PEAK DISTRICT PLACE NAMES by Martin Spray

JOHN MERRILL'S MAJOR WALKS -
TURN RIGHT AT LAND'S END
WITH MUSTARD ON MY BACK
TURN RIGHT AT DEATH VALLEY
EMERALD COAST WALK

COLOUR GUIDES -
THE PEAK DISTRICT.........Something to remember her by.

SKETCH BOOKS -
NORTH STAFFORDSHIRE SKETCHBOOK by John Creber
SKETCHES OF THE PEAK DISTRICT

IN PREPARATION -
LONG CIRCULAR WALKS IN STAFFORDSHIRE
SHORT CIRCULAR WALKS IN THE YORKSHIRE DALES
SHORT CIRCULAR WALKS IN THE LAKE DISTRICT
SHORT CIRCULAR WALKS IN NORTH YORKSHIRE MOORS
SNOWDONIA CHALLENGE WALK
FOOTPATHS OF THE WORLD - Vol 1 - NORTH AMERICA
HIKING IN NEW MEXICO - 5 VOLUMES

☞ **Full list from JNM PUBLICATIONS, Winster, Matlock, Derbys.**